COOKBOOK

SWAP YOUR FAVORITE RECIPES WITH NUTRIENT DENSE CAULIFLOWER TO CREATE DELICIOUS **LOW CARB** HEALTHY ALTERNATIVES

Published by The Fruitful Mind
www.fruitfulbooks.com

Disclaimer

Table of Contents

Introduction

Following a low carb diet is easier than you think. You can substitute many high carb foods like potatoes and pasta with a low carb food instead. This book contains many popular recipes where cauliflower has been substituted to lower the carb count. The recipes are still delicious and healthier for you!

A low carb diet is the best way to lose weight and keep it off. On this type of diet you cut out all of the processed foods, which are not good for you anyway. All of the recipes in this book use only whole, natural ingredients. You will also be eliminating food items high in sugar, or sugar substitutes, which only pack on the pounds. As you follow this diet you will find your energy increasing, your overall health improving and you will sleep better at night.

If you suffer from diabetes, either Type 1 or 2, this diet will help you to control your sugar levels. Your body turns every carb you eat into sugar. Many people with diabetes do not know this fact. They tend to focus only on the amount of sugar they are eating and not controlling their carb intake.

The recipes in this book focus on a little known super food; cauliflower. You can substitute any high carb food with this easy to use vegetable. Use it to make your pasta gluten free, your breads and pizzas low carb and a healthier version of the popular mashed potatoes.

Cauliflower is high in antioxidants, minerals and vitamins. Just one serving of cauliflower contains about 77% of the recommended daily dose of

Vitamin C. Studies have shown that this vegetable is beneficial in fighting cancer, inflammation and digestive issues. Eating cauliflower will help improve brain function, improve heart health and even reduce stress.

This handy book contains more than enough recipes to get you started on your low carb diet. You will find snack recipes like Choco Flower Brownies. Soup recipes for lunch or dinner like Just Like Potato. Learn how to make Cauliflower Rice in the chapter on side dishes. And you can even use cauliflower in your entrees, try the Green Chili Enchilada Casserole made with chicken. So good even the kids will eat them. Enjoy!

Cauliflower
🌾 SNACK
RECIPES

Baked Cheesy Puffs

Satisfy your craving for muffins, or almost any baked treat, with these low carb cheese puffs. They make a great grab-and-go snack.

Prep time 23 minutes

Cooking time 22 minutes

Ingredients:

1 medium head cauliflower, separated into small florets

3 cloves garlic, chopped fine

½ cup sharp cheddar cheese, grated

1/3 cup sour cream

1 tablespoon dried parsley

3/4 teaspoon salt

1/4 teaspoon pepper

2 large eggs

2 egg whites

Directions:

Preheat oven to 400 degrees. Lightly grease a non-stick muffin or cornbread baking pan.

In a medium saucepan, over medium heat, cook cauliflower and garlic, in a couple of inches of water, about 8-10 minutes or till very tender. Drain.

Place the cauliflower, along with the garlic, into a blender. Pulse till smooth. Transfer the mixture to a large bowl.

Add cheese, sour cream and parsley. Mix together then add salt and pepper to taste. Add 2 whole eggs and mix well.

In a medium bowl, beat the egg whites till stiff. Be careful not to over beat them, they should not be dry. Fold the egg whites gently into the cauliflower mixture just till the ingredients are combined.

Spoon the batter into the prepared muffin or cornbread pan. Bake in the oven for 18-22 minutes till light brown. Remove from oven and serve.

Serves 12

Nutritional information: Serving size 1 muffin

80 Calories; 5g Fat; 3g Carbs; 5g Protein

Buffalo Cauliflower "Wings"

All of the flavor of Buffalo wings without all the fat and calories. Perfect for an afternoon snack or while watching your favorite game on TV.

Prep time 5 minutes

Cooking time 20 minutes

Ingredients:

1 large head of cauliflower, separated into small florets

3 tablespoons olive oil

1 teaspoon garlic salt

1/8 teaspoon pepper

2 tablespoons melted butter

2/3 cup wing sauce

Directions:

Heat oven to 450F degrees.

In a medium bowl, place cauliflower and drizzle with oil. Toss to coat. Add garlic salt and pepper. Toss to coat evenly.

Place on an ungreased cooking sheet. Bake for 15 minutes; turning florets once after 5 minutes. Check after 10 minutes for desired doneness.

Melt butter in a glass bowl in the microwave. Add hot sauce to butter and whisk to combine. Remove cauliflower from oven and toss them in the hot sauce to coat evenly.

Return them to the cooking sheet and bake for an additional 5 minutes.

Serve with low carb ranch or blue cheese dressing for dipping.

Serves 4

Nutritional information: Serving size about ¾ cup

190 Calories; 16g Fat; 9g Carbs; 4g Protein

Choco-Flower Brownies

Bet you didn't know you could eat fudgy brownies on a low carb diet. Well with this recipe you can. They are low in calories too so don't have to feel guilty if you eat more than one.

Prep Time 20 minutes

Cooking time 35 minutes

Ingredients:

1 cup raw cauliflower puree

½ cup unsweetened almond milk

½ cup butter

2 ounces cream cheese, softened

6 squares good quality dark chocolate

⅓ cup unsweetened chocolate syrup

3 eggs

1 cup ground almonds

½ cup coconut flour

½ cup unsweetened cocoa powder

3 teaspoon honey

2 teaspoon ground cinnamon

½ teaspoon baking powder

⅛ teaspoon salt

Directions:

Preheat oven to 375 degrees. Lightly grease a 9x9 baking pan.

Cut up the cauliflower and remove the core and any leaves. Place the cauliflower in a blender or food processor and puree. Add almond milk and process till smooth, about 30 seconds.

Put the butter, cream cheese and chocolate squares into a microwave safe bowl and microwave for one minute.

Add the chocolate mixture to the blender with the cauliflower. Process for about 20 seconds till well blended. Add the chocolate syrup and eggs and blend well.

In a large bowl, combine all of the dry ingredients. Add the chocolate mix from the blender and stir till ingredients are thoroughly combined. The batter should be thick.

Pour the batter into the baking pan. Bake at 375 degrees for 35 minutes. Remove from oven and let cool. Cut into 1 ½ inch squares.

Makes 36 brownies

Nutritional information: Serving size 1 brownie

70 Calories; 6g Fat; 4g Carbs; 2g Protein

"Faux" Rice Pudding

Sometimes you just have to satisfy your craving for something sweet. Diet or no diet. Here is the perfect treat when those cravings sneak up on you. Low carb cauliflower "rice" pudding.

Prep time 10 minutes

Cooking time 10 minutes

Ingredients:

¾ cup cauliflower, grated

¾ cup milk

¾ cup sugar

1 teaspoon vanilla

¾ cup cream cheese, room temperature

1 cinnamon stick

Cinnamon, for garnish

Directions:

Place the cauliflower, 1/3 cup milk, sugar and vanilla into a medium glass bowl. Microwave about 2 minutes. Remove from microwave and let rest about 10-15 minutes.

Add the remaining milk with the cream cheese and cinnamon stick to a medium sauce pot. Cook, stirring constantly, over medium high heat till the cheese has melted and the mixture resembles pudding.

Discard the cinnamon stick and add the cauliflower. Stir till all the ingredients are combined thoroughly.

Pour the pudding into 5 serving cups or bowls. Sprinkle the top with cinnamon. Cover and refrigerate for 2-4 hours before serving.

Serves 5

Nutritional information: Serving size 1 dish

164 Calories; 12g Fat; 10g Carbs; 4g Protein

Garlic "Bread" Sticks

Serve these yummy "bread" sticks with your favorite low carb marinara sauce for dipping. Just like the tasty bread sticks you get from any of the pizza restaurants but low carb and gluten free.

Prep time 15 minutes

Cooking time 15 minutes

Ingredients:

1 head of cauliflower, trimmed and grated

¼ + ½ cup of mozzarella cheese

¼ cup of parmesan cheese

1 teaspoon basil

1 teaspoon oregano

½ teaspoon pepper

½ teaspoon garlic salt

¼ tsp red pepper flakes

1 egg

Directions:

Heat oven to 450 degrees. Line a large baking sheet with parchment paper.

Put the cauliflower in a medium glass bowl and cover. Cook in the microwave about 2-3 minutes. Let it cool completely.

When the cauliflower has cooled, use paper towels, a cheese cloth, or your hands to squeeze the water out of it. You want it to be as dry as possible.

In a medium mixing bowl, add the cauliflower, ¼ cup mozzarella cheese, parmesan and seasonings. Stir to combine all of the ingredients together.

Add the egg and stir to combine. Using your hands, form the mixture into a ball. Place the dough on the paper lined baking sheet and spread it to cover the pan. Making sure it is in a nice even layer.

Bake 10-15 minutes or till a light, toasty brown. Sprinkle the ½ cup of mozzarella cheese over the top and return to the oven. Bake another 5-7 minutes till cheese has melted.

Remove from oven and cool slightly before cutting. Cut into ½ inch strips and serve.

Serves 6

Nutritional information: Serving size approximately 3 slices

260 Calories; 18g Fat; 7g Carbs; 18g Protein

Oven Fried Cauliflower Bites

These are perfect for snacking. Light and crispy and so much healthier than potato chips. Fair warning, they are highly addictive.

Prep time 10 minutes

Cooking time 30 minutes

Ingredients:

4 cups cauliflower, separated into small florets

1 tablespoon olive oil

1/2 teaspoon garlic salt

1 egg, lightly beaten

1/2 cup parmesan cheese, grated

Directions:

Heat oven to 400 degrees. Lightly grease a large cookie sheet with olive oil.

Put the cauliflower florets in a large glass mixing bowl.

Lightly beat the egg with the garlic salt in a small mixing bowl. Pour over the cauliflower and stir to mix thoroughly.

Sprinkle the cheese over the vegetables and mix being sure to coat all of the florets.

Spread the cauliflower, in a single layer, on the prepared cookie sheet. Bake 20-30 minutes till golden brown and cauliflower is tender.

Serves 4

Nutritional information: Serving size 1 cup

135 Calories; 9g Fat; 6g Carbs; 9g Protein

Cauliflower SOUP RECIPES

Bacon Burger Soup

Who doesn't love a juicy, grilled bacon cheese burger? But what about all that fat and those calories? Don't fret, get that same great taste in this low carb soup. Perfect for lunch or dinner on those cool autumn days.

Prep time 5 minutes

Cooking time 20 minutes

Ingredients

1 pound lean ground beef

6 strips bacon, cooked crisp and crumbled

1 head Cauliflower, separated into florets

3 1/2 cups vegetable broth

1 cup milk

1 teaspoon parsley

3/4 teaspoon kosher salt

1/4 teaspoon pepper

2 cups cheddar cheese, grated

1/2 cup heavy cream

Directions:

In a large sauce pot, over medium high heat, cook ground beef till done, about 8-10 minutes.

Add the bacon, cauliflower, vegetable broth, milk and seasonings and bring to a boil.

Decrease heat to medium and continue cooking 10-15 minutes or until cauliflower is soft. Turn off the heat and stir in cheese and cream till the cheese has melted. Serve warm.

Serves 8

Nutritional information: Serving size about 1 cup

420 Calories; 29g Fat; 9g Carbs; 28g Protein

Crab & Cauliflower Bisque

Smooth and creamy, this is comfort food at its best. You can use canned crab in this recipe but go for fresh if you can.

Prep time 20 minutes

Cooking time 30 minutes

Ingredients:

4 tablespoons butter

1 cup celery, chopped fine

1 white onion, chopped fine

1 cup carrots, chopped fine

1 medium head cauliflower, separated into very small florets

6 cups chicken broth

1½ teaspoon coarse salt

1 teaspoon white pepper

1 cup heavy cream

1 tablespoon sherry

1 pound lump crabmeat, cooked and shells removed

Directions:

Melt butter in a large saucepan over medium high heat. Place the celery, onion and carrot in the pot. Cook, stirring frequently, till the vegetables are soft.

Add in the cauliflower, broth, salt and pepper and continue cooking till soup starts to boil. Reduce the heat to medium and continue cooking about 15 minutes or until cauliflower is soft.

Pour the soup into a blender and add the cream and sherry. Pulse till the ingredients are combined and soup is smooth. Pour back into saucepan.

Gently fold in the crab meat and cook just till the soup is warm again. Ladle into bowls and serve.

Serves 8

Nutritional information: Serving size about 1 ¼ cups

290 Calories; 21g Fat; 10g Carbs; 17g Protein

Creamy Broccoli & Cauliflower Soup

Perfect meal when you want something light but filling. Both broccoli and cauliflower are great sources of fiber without a lot of calories.

Prep time 15 minutes

Cooking time 15 minutes

Ingredients:

1 head broccoli, separated into florets

1 head cauliflower, separated into florets

1 teaspoon olive oil

1 tablespoon garlic, peeled and chopped fine

1 shallot, sliced thin

2½ cups milk

¼ cup parmesan cheese, grated

¼ teaspoon salt

black pepper

Directions:

Fill a large stock pot with water and bring to a boil over medium high heat. When the water begins to boil add the broccoli and cauliflower and cook 8-10 minutes or till vegetables are tender. Remove from heat and drain well.

In a small frying pan, over medium low heat, heat the oil. Add the garlic and shallot and cook till soft, about 4-5 minutes.

Add the broccoli and cauliflower, garlic and shallots, milk and cheese to a blender. Process at high speed till the mixture is smooth and creamy. Season with salt and pepper to taste.

Return the mixture to the stock pot and heat through over medium heat, about 5 minutes. Serve.

Serves 10

Nutritional information: Serving size about 1 ¼ cups

80 Calories; 8g Fat; 10g Carbs; 6g Protein

Easy Clam Chowder

Here is a great recipe that uses the core of the cauliflower. So save the core from other recipes and try this super easy soup for a quick meal that is ready in less than 30 minutes.

Prep time 5 minutes

Cooking time 15 minutes

Ingredients:

2 cups heavy cream

2 cups vegetable broth

1 core of a fresh head of cauliflower, cut into bite size pieces

1 tablespoon minced onion

10 ounce can clams and broth

1 tablespoon butter

1/2 teaspoon minced parsley

Directions:

Pour the cream and broth into a medium saucepan. Heat over medium high heat just till the mixture starts to boil. Add the cauliflower and onions.

Cook, uncovered, about 10 minutes or until cauliflower is soft. Add the remaining ingredients to the pan and cook about 5 minutes more, stirring frequently. Serve.

Serves 6

Nutritional information: Serving size about 1 ¼ cups

410 Calories; 38g Fat; 10g Carbs; 10g Protein

Greek Chicken Soup

This soup is similar to the classic Greek Lemon Soup. Chicken with cauliflower "rice" and tangy hint of lemon. This is a perfect comfort food for those cool days of early spring.

Prep time 15 minutes

Cooking time 15 minutes

Ingredients:

1/2 medium head cauliflower, grated

1 tablespoon olive oil

1/2 onion, chopped fine

1 teaspoon garlic salt

6 cups chicken broth

1 bay leaf

1 pound chicken, cooked and cut into bite size pieces

1/3 cup lemon juice

1 large egg

Salt and pepper to taste

Directions:

Heat the oil in a large sauce pot over medium heat. Add the onion to the pot and cook 4-5 minutes or till the onion is tender. Add in the chicken broth and bay leaf and cook till the mixture begins to boil.

Decrease the heat and place the chicken and cauliflower in the pot. Cook about 10 minutes, stirring occasionally, till cauliflower is tender.

Beat the lemon juice and egg together in a medium bowl. Add 1 cup of the hot soup, pouring it slowly while beating the mixture continuously. Add the lemon egg mixture to the pot.

Remove the bay leaf. Taste the soup and season with salt and pepper. Serve while hot.

Serves 6

Nutritional information: Serving size about 1 cup
280 Calories; 16g Fat; 8g Carbs; 28g Protein

Ham & Cauliflower Soup

Delicious, warm and filling, just what a good soup should be. This recipe is quick to make and a great way to use up left over ham.

Prep time 10 minutes

Cooking time 40 minutes

Ingredients:

1 large head cauliflower, separated into florets

6 cups chicken broth

2 cups water

2 tablespoons onion, chopped fine

2 tablespoons garlic, chopped fine

3 cups ham, cut into bite size pieces

1 tablespoon fresh thyme

1-2 drops Liquid Smoke

2 tablespoons apple cider vinegar

2 tablespoons coconut oil

Salt and pepper to taste

Directions:

In a large stock pot, over medium high heat, combine cauliflower, broth, water, onion and garlic. Bring to boil and cook about 25-30 minutes.

Use an immersion blender to blend the soup in the pot, or pour small amounts in a blender and process till smooth. Add the mixture back to the pot.

Add the ham, thyme and Liquid Smoke and continue cooking another 10 minutes. Turn off the heat and stir in vinegar and coconut oil till combined and coconut oil is melted. Season with salt and pepper to taste. Serve.

Serves 10

Nutritional information: Serving size 1½ cups

80 Calories; 4g Fat; 6g Carbs; 5g Protein

Just Like Potato Soup

When the nights get cool nothing satisfies like a warm, creamy bowl of soup. This low carb, gluten free soup is related to the popular potato one, but so much better for you.

Prep time 10 minutes

Cooking time 15 minutes

Ingredients:

1 tablespoon olive oil

¼ cup white onion, chopped fine

2 garlic cloves, peeled and chopped fine

1 head cauliflower, separated into florets

4 - 5 cups vegetable broth

Salt and pepper

3 strips bacon, cooked crisp and crumbled

1 green onion, sliced thin

Directions:

Heat the oil in a medium saucepan over medium high heat. Add the onion and cook about 5 minutes till softened. Add the garlic and stir and cook one more minute.

Add the cauliflower and broth to the pan. Bring the mixture to a boil. Cover and reduce heat. Cook for 10-15 minutes or till the cauliflower is very tender.

Pour the soup into a blender and process till smooth and creamy. Transfer the soup back to the pan and reheat, about 1 minute. Add salt and pepper to taste.

Spoon soup into serving bowls and top with crumbled bacon and sliced green onion.

Serves 4

Nutritional information: Serving size about 1 cup

90 Calories; 3g Fat; 13g Carbs; 3g Protein

Roasted Cauliflower Soup

This soup recipe only has five ingredients. Super simple to make and sure to impress your family and friends. The soup tastes like one you would expect to find in a fine dining restaurant.

Prep time 5 minutes

Cooking time 1 hour 45 minutes

Ingredients

1 large head cauliflower, trimmed

4 tablespoons extra virgin olive oil

1 teaspoon coarse salt

½ cup water

1 large onion, chopped fine

4 cups vegetable broth

Directions:

Heat the oven to 350 degrees. Rub 2 tablespoons of the olive oil over the cauliflower and sprinkle with salt. Place the cauliflower in a 13x9 baking pan. Pour the water into the pan around the cauliflower.

Bake 1½ hours or till the middle of the cauliflower is tender. Remove from oven and cool completely.

When the cauliflower has cooled chop into small pieces. Add the remaining olive oil to a large sauce pot and heat over medium heat.

Add the onion and cook about 10 minutes or till the onion is tender. Add the chopped cauliflower and broth to the pot. Simmer, over medium heat for 10 minutes.

Pour the soup into a blender and process till smooth so no chunks of cauliflower remain. Pour back into the sauce pot and heat through. Serve.

Serves 4

Nutritional information: Serving size about 1 ½ cups

170 Calories; 14g Fat; 10g Carbs; 3g Protein

Cauliflower
SIDE DISHES
RECIPES

Almost Mac 'N Cheese

Just like the baked mac and cheese your mom or grandma used to make. Instead of the traditional macaroni this low carb recipe uses cauliflower. The dish cooks up with the same texture and yummy flavor. The kids will love it, just don't tell them it's cauliflower!

Prep time 10 minutes

Cooking time 15 minutes

Ingredients:

1 large head cauliflower, separated into small florets

1 cup heavy cream

¼ cup cream cheese, room temperature

1 1/2 teaspoons mustard powder

1/4 teaspoon pepper

1/8 teaspoon garlic salt

1 1/2 cups cheddar cheese, grated

Directions:

Heat oven to 375 degrees. Lightly oil an 8x8 inch glass baking dish. Cook the cauliflower in large pot of boiling, salted water about 5 minutes. Cauliflower should be tender-crisp, not too soft.

Drain water and place cauliflower on a paper towel lined sheet to absorb any excess water. Place the cauliflower in the prepared baking dish.

In a small sauce pot, over medium heat, heat the heavy cream to a simmer. Stir in the cream cheese and mustard powder. Stir continuously till mixture is smooth.

Add in pepper, garlic salt and 1½ cups of the cheddar cheese. Continue stirring and cooking till all of the cheese is melted.

Remove from heat and immediately pour over the cauliflower in the baking dish. Gently stir to combine the cauliflower and cheese sauce evenly.

Sprinkle the remaining ½ cup cheddar cheese over the top.

Bake 15 minutes or till the cheese is bubbly and golden brown. Serve.

Serves 6

Nutritional information: Serving size about ½ cup

340 Calories; 30g Fat; 7g Carbs; 11g Protein

Bacon & Jalapeno Cauliflower

Inspired from the popular jalapeno poppers. Layers of cauliflower, creamy cheese, spicy jalapenos and, of course, bacon. Serve this as a side dish or with a salad as the main course. Either way, it's a winner.

Prep time 20 minutes

Cooking time 20 minutes

Ingredients:

1 head of cauliflower, separated into small florets

2 tablespoons heavy cream

1 tablespoon butter

3/4 cup sharp cheddar cheese, grated

1 tablespoon raw jalapeno pepper, seeded and chopped fine

¼ tsp garlic powder

Salt and pepper to taste

¾ cup cream cheese, room temperature

¼ cup green chili sauce

¾ cup Colby jack cheese, grated

51

4 strips bacon, cooked crisp and crumbled

¼ cup jalapeno peppers, seeded and cut into strips

Directions:

Heat oven to 375 degrees.

Place the cauliflower, butter and cream into a medium sauce pan. Cook over medium heat, stirring frequently, till mixture comes to a simmer. Simmer, uncovered, 15 minutes or till cauliflower is soft.

Put the cauliflower into a blender along with ¼ cup cheese, chopped jalapeno peppers and garlic powder. Process till smooth and no chunks remain. Season with salt and pepper. Spread the mixture evenly in an 8x8 inch baking pan.

Beat cream cheese, ½ cup cheddar cheese and green chili sauce together in a medium mixing bowl. The mixture should be smooth and easy to spread. Spread over the cauliflower layer in the baking pan.

Sprinkle the top with the Colby jack cheese, crumbled bacon and sliced jalapeno peppers. Bake 20 minutes or till bubbly and the cheese is melted and golden brown. Serve hot.

Serves 6

Nutritional information: Serving size ½ cup

290 Calories; 28g Fat; 9g Carbs; 14g Protein

Cauliflower "Rice"

Rice is a staple found in many countries. Replace the rice in any of your favorite dishes with this low carb cauliflower version. It has the same texture but is healthier than its namesake.

Prep time 5 minutes

Cooking time 10 minutes

Ingredients:

1 small head cauliflower, separated into small florets

1 tablespoon olive oil

1 clove of garlic, peeled and chopped fine

½ teaspoon salt

Directions:

To make cauliflower rice use a cheese grater or food processor. If you are using a cheese grater, grate the cauliflower over the big holes.

If you are using a food processor, the quickest method, process the cauliflower till it resembles grains of rice.

Add the olive oil to a nonstick skillet and heat over medium high heat. Add the garlic and cook 1 minute, stirring frequently.

Add the cauliflower and continue to cook, stirring frequently, about 7-9 minutes. The cauliflower should be tender and a nice toasty brown color. Serve as is or use the rice in another recipe.

Serves 4

Nutritional information: Serving size about ¾ cup 70 Calories; 3g Fat; 8g Carbs; 3g Protein

Cauliflower Risotto

All the flavors you love in the traditional Italian side dish. Without all the calories and carbs you hate.

Ingredients:

2 tablespoons extra virgin olive oil

4 cups cauliflower, grated

1 cup mushrooms, stems removed and sliced thin

½ cup onion, chopped fine

½ cup green peas

½ cup asparagus, cut into very small pieces

2 cloves garlic, peeled and chopped fine

¼ cup dry white wine

½ cup milk

½ cup vegetable broth

½ cup parmesan cheese, grated

½ teaspoon salt

¼ teaspoon pepper

Zest of 1 lemon

Directions:

In a large, deep skillet, over medium-high heat, heat half the oil. Add mushrooms and cook, stirring frequently, about 3 minutes, or till tender. Remove the mushrooms and set aside.

Reduce the heat to medium. Add remaining olive oil to the skillet along with the onions and garlic. Cook, stirring frequently, about 3-4 minutes.

Add the cauliflower and stir to mix all the ingredients thoroughly. Cook for an additional 1 to 2 minutes.

Pour in the white wine, stir continuously and continue cooking about 2 minutes or till the wine is evaporated.

Add the asparagus and peas and mix them into the other ingredients. Increase the heat to medium-high.

Add the milk and vegetable broth and cook, stirring occasionally, about 6-8 minutes, till the cauliflower is softened and most of the liquid has evaporated.

Remove from heat and add cheese, mushrooms and lemon zest. Mix thoroughly. Season with salt and pepper to taste. Serve.

Serves 4

Nutritional information: Serving size about 1 cup

152 Calories; 8g Fat; 14g Carbs; 6g Protein

Creamy Shrimp & Black Olive Salad

No one likes to eat a heavy meal during the hot months of summer. Make this delicious, low carb version of a popular pasta salad for lunch. Or show it off at that summer BBQ or potluck.

Prep time 15 minutes

Cooking time 10 minutes

Ingredients:

For the salad:

5 cups cauliflower, separated into small florets

1 pound large shrimp, deveined and cooked

½ cup black olives, sliced

⅓ cup celery, chopped

1 tablespoon fresh dill, chopped coarse

For the dressing:

½ cup mayonnaise

¼ teaspoon celery seed

2 tablespoons fresh lemon juice

2 teaspoons sugar

1 teaspoon apple cider vinegar

¼ tsp sea salt

⅛ teaspoon pepper

Directions:

Cook the cauliflower in a large pot of boiling, salted water. Drain well and refrigerate 1-2 hours. Make sure the shrimp is chilled as well.

In a large salad bowl combine cauliflower, shrimp, olives, celery and dill. Mix well.

In a small mixing bowl, stir together mayonnaise, celery seed, lemon juice, sugar, vinegar, salt and pepper. Mix till smooth and the sugar is completely dissolved.

Pour the dressing over the salad ingredients and toss together. Cover and refrigerate 1-2 hours to allow the flavors to combine. Serve cold.

Serves 8

Nutritional information: Serving size 1 cup

70 Calories; 6g Fat; 5g Carbs; 0g Protein

Fried "Rice"

This recipe is super versatile. Use up that left over chicken by adding it to the dish and voila, Chicken Fried Rice. Or serve it as a base for your favorite Asian dish.

Prep time 5 minutes

Cooking time 10 minutes

Ingredients:

2 tablespoons vegetable oil

2 eggs, beat lightly

2 garlic cloves, peeled and chopped fine

1 large head cauliflower, grated

1/2 cup corn kernels

1/2 cup peas

1 tablespoon soy sauce, or to taste

Directions:

Add 1 tablespoon of oil to a large skillet and heat over medium heat. Pour in the eggs and cook to a soft scramble. Remove from the skillet.

Add the remaining oil to the skillet along with the garlic. Cook about 1 minute.

Add the cauliflower and cook, stirring constantly, 1-2 minutes. Add the eggs back to the skillet and continue cooking and stirring for an additional 2 minutes.

Add the corn, peas and soy sauce and cook, stirring often, 4-5 minutes or till the cauliflower is tender. Serve.

Serves 4

Nutritional information: Serving size about ¾ cup

130 Calories; 10g Fat; 7g Carbs; 5g Protein

Garlic Parmesan Roasted Cauliflower

Super simple to make and so delicious to eat. Makes the perfect substitute for those roasted potatoes you used to make.

Prep time 10 minutes

Cooking time 25 minutes

Ingredients:

1 medium head cauliflower, cut into florets

3 large cloves garlic, minced

1/4 cup olive oil

2 tablespoons lemon juice

1/2 teaspoon salt

1/4 teaspoon black pepper

2 tablespoons grated Parmesan cheese

Directions:

Heat oven to 450 degrees F. In a large bowl combine cauliflower and garlic.

In a small bowl, whisk together the oil, lemon juice, salt and pepper. Drizzle over the cauliflower and mix to coat evenly.

Place on a large baking sheet in a single layer. Bake 25 minutes stirring halfway through baking time.

Sprinkle with cheese and serve immediately.

Serves 4

Nutritional information: Serving size about ¾ cup

180 Calories; 14g Fat; 9g Carbs; 4g Protein

Mock Mashed "Potatoes"

Mashed potatoes are a traditional side dish that go well with just about everything. Try substituting those high carb potatoes with cauliflower for a low carb side that tastes delicious.

Prep time 10 minutes

Cooking time 8 minutes

Ingredients:

1 medium head cauliflower, separated into florets and steamed

4 tablespoons butter, melted

2 teaspoons garlic, chopped fine

½ teaspoon onion powder

½ teaspoon salt

¼ teaspoon pepper

Directions:

Place the cauliflower, butter and garlic into a blender or food processor. Pulse till the ingredients are smooth and resemble mashed potatoes. Scrape the sides of the blender or processor as needed.

Add onion powder, salt and pepper to taste. Stir to mix in the seasonings and transfer to serving bowl. Serve immediately.

Serves 4

Nutritional information: Serving size about ½ cup

140 Calories; 12g Fat; 9g Carbs; 3g Protein

Twice Baked Cheesy Cauliflower

Similar in taste to twice baked potatoes. Loaded with all of the same flavors but a lot less carbs and cooking time.

Prep time 10 minutes

Cooking time 40 minutes

Ingredients:

1 large head cauliflower, separated into small florets

6 strips of bacon, cooked crisp and crumbled

1/2 cup sour cream

½ cup cream cheese, room temperature

1/4 cup Parmesan cheese, grated

1/4 cup green onions, chopped fine

1 cup sharp cheddar cheese, grated

Directions:

Heat oven to 350 degrees.

Heat a large pan of salted water to a boil. Add cauliflower and cook about 10 minutes or till tender. Drain well and transfer to a large bowl. Using a potato masher, mash the cauliflower till mostly smooth, leave some small pieces.

Add the sour cream, cream cheese, Parmesan cheese, green onions and ¾ of the bacon. Stir well to thoroughly combine all ingredients.

Spread the mixture evenly in a 2 quart casserole dish. Sprinkle the cheddar cheese and remaining bacon over the top. Cover and bake 25 minutes.

Remove the cover and continue baking another 5-10 minutes or till cheese is bubbly and golden brown.

Serves 6

Nutritional information: Serving size about ¾ cup

320 Calories; 16g Fat; 6g Carbs; 11g Protein

Cauliflower

MAIN COURSES
RECIPES

Breakfast Casserole

Make this for a weekend breakfast or brunch. The flavor is so good no one will miss the usual hash browns found in a baked breakfast casserole.

Prep time 15 minutes

Cooking time 30 minutes

Ingredients:

1 pound pork sausage

8 strips of bacon

2 cups cauliflower, separated into small florets

1 green bell pepper, chopped into small pieces

½ cup onions, chopped fine

½ teaspoon salt

½ teaspoon pepper

1 teaspoon garlic powder

11 eggs

1 teaspoon hot pepper sauce

1 cup sharp cheddar cheese

Directions:

Heat oven to 350 degrees. Lightly oil 13x9 inch baking dish.

Add the cauliflower to a medium saucepan of boiling salted water. Cook about 8 minutes or till cauliflower is tender. Drain well.

In a large frying pan, cook the bacon and sausage till done. Remove the bacon and sausage and drain on paper towels. Pour the grease from the pan. Crumble meat into small pieces.

Return the frying pan to the stove and cook the onions and peppers, over medium high heat, just till the green pepper starts to get soft.

Turn the heat off and add the cauliflower, meat and seasonings to the pan. Stir to combine the ingredients. Spread the cauliflower mixture in the prepared pan.

In a large mixing bowl, beat the eggs with the hot pepper sauce. Do not over beat. Pour over the vegetable mix in the baking dish. Sprinkle the cheddar cheese on top.

Bake 30-35 minutes or till the eggs are completely set and the cheese is melted. Remove from the oven and let stand 3-5 minutes before cutting. Cut into 8 slices and serve.

Serves 8

Nutritional information: Serving size 1 slice

360 Calories; 31g Fat; 4g Carbs; 18g Protein

Cauliflower Pizza Crust

If you like a crispy crust on your pizza, this may not appeal to you. But the crust is delicious and makes a nice low carb alternative when you are craving a slice of pizza. Add your favorite sauce, toppings and cheese and eat pizza without any guilt.

Prep time 15 minutes

Cooking time 25 minutes

Ingredients:

1 tablespoon extra-virgin olive oil

2 tablespoons butter

1 large head cauliflower, separated into small florets

1/3 cup white onion, chopped fine

1/4 cup water

3 eggs

2 cups mozzarella cheese, grated and run through food processor

2 teaspoons Italian seasoning

1/4 cup parmesan cheese, grated

Directions:

Heat oven to 450 degrees. Use the olive oil to grease a large baking sheet.

Melt the butter in a large frying pan over medium heat. Add the onion and cauliflower and cook till cauliflower starts to get soft, about 10 minutes.

Add the water and cover the pan. Continue cooking till the cauliflower is soft, about 5 minutes. Remove from heat. Let cool completely.

When the cauliflower is cool place 3 cups into a blender or food processor. Pulse till the mixture is smooth. Transfer the mixture to a large mixing bowl.

To the bowl add eggs, both cheeses and the seasonings. Stir well to combine the ingredients.

Spread the batter onto the prepared baking sheet in an even layer. Bake about 20 minutes till golden brown on the edges.

Turn the oven to broil. Spread the crust with your favorite sauce and add toppings.

Sprinkle with additional grated cheese and broil about 5 minutes or till cheese has melted. Remove from oven, cut into squares and serve.

Serves 4

Nutritional information: Serving size 2 slices

250 Calories; 18g Fat; 10g Carbs; 14g Protein

Cheeseburger Cauliflower

This recipe is based on those cheeseburger pasta dishes. Same great taste but instead of using a high carb pasta, use low carb cauliflower instead. Great dinner idea when you are short on time.

Prep time 10 minutes

Cooking time 15 minutes

Ingredients:

1 large head cauliflower, separated into small florets

1 1/2 pounds lean ground beef

1 cup mushrooms, stems removed and sliced

1 small green pepper, seeded and cut into small pieces

¼ cup onion, chopped fine

1 cup cheddar cheese

1/2 teaspoon garlic powder

Salt and pepper, to taste

Directions:

Cook cauliflower in a large pot of boiling salted water for about 10 minutes or till tender. Drain well.

In a large frying pan, over medium high heat, fry the ground beef till almost done. Drain off the grease. Add the mushrooms, green pepper and onion to the pan and cook till the onion is translucent and the peppers are tender.

Add cauliflower, cheese and garlic powder. Stir to combine all the ingredients in the pan. Continue cooking just till cheese is melted. Add salt and pepper to taste. Serve.

Serves 6

Nutritional information: Serving size about ¾ cup

340 Calories; 23g Fat; 5g Carbs; 28g Protein

Classic Shepherd's Pie

A low carb version of a great comfort food. Perfect for dinner on a cold winter night. This hearty dish tastes wonderful and it is guilt free.

Prep time 30 minutes

Cooking time 25 minutes

Ingredients:

1 head of cauliflower, separated into florets

¼ cup of heavy cream

2 tablespoons butter, melted

¾ teaspoon salt

¼ teaspoon pepper

1 pound lean ground beef

1 tablespoon coconut oil

1 medium onion, chopped fine

1 cup mushrooms, sliced

1 medium carrot, cut into small pieces

1 tablespoon tomato paste

¼ cup red wine

Dash of Worcestershire sauce

2 teaspoons garlic, chopped fine

1 teaspoon rosemary

1 teaspoon thyme

½ tablespoon of cornstarch

½ cup cheddar cheese, grated

Directions:

Heat oven to 400 degrees. Lightly grease a 2 quart glass baking dish.

Place cauliflower into large pot of boiling, salted water. Cook about 10 minutes or till the cauliflower is tender. Drain well.

Put the cauliflower into a blender and add cream and butter. Process till smooth and no chunks remain. Season with salt and pepper.

Heat the oil in a large frying pan over medium heat. Add the onion, mushrooms and carrots. Cook, stirring occasionally, till vegetables are tender, about 8-10 minutes. Using a slotted spoon, remove the vegetables from the pan and place in a bowl.

Add the ground beef to the pan and cook, breaking up it up with a spoon, till the beef is nicely browned, about 4-5 minutes.

Add the vegetables, tomato paste, wine, Worcestershire, garlic and seasonings to the beef. Decrease the heat to low and cook for 10 minutes, stirring occasionally. Add the cornstarch and stir well. Remove from heat.

Pour the meat mixture into the prepared baking dish. Spoon the cauliflower puree on top being sure to cover the meat mixture completely.

Sprinkle the top of the casserole with cheese. Bake 25 minutes, till bubbly and cheese is melted and lightly browned.

Serves 6

Nutritional information: Serving size about 1 ½ cups

400 Calories; 28g Fat; 12g Carbs; 23g Protein

Fiesta Casserole

Make this yummy casserole when you are in the mood for something spicy. All the traditional flavors of your favorite Mexican dish but so better for you.

Prep time 15 minutes

Cooking time 30 minutes

Ingredients:

½ white onion, chopped fine

1 red bell pepper, seeded and chopped fine

1 green bell pepper, seeded and chopped fine

1 jalapeno pepper, seeded and chopped fine

1 teaspoon cilantro, chopped fine

1 teaspoon chili powder

1 head cauliflower, grated

3 tablespoons water

½ cup salsa

1½ cups cheddar cheese, grated

Directions:

Heat the oven to 350 degrees. Lightly grease 7x11x2 inch baking pan.

In a large frying pan, over medium heat, cook onions and peppers till softened, about 4-5 minutes. Add in the cilantro and chili powder and stir to combine. Remove from heat.

Place the grated cauliflower and water in a microwavable safe bowl and microwave on high for about 3 minutes. Stir in 1 cup of the cheese and the salsa.

Add the pepper mixture to the cauliflower mixture and stir together. Spread in the baking pan. Top with remaining ½ cup of cheese and bake 30-35 minutes.

Remove from oven and let sit 5 minutes. Cut into 12 squares.

Serves 12

Nutritional information: Serving size 1 square

80 Calories; 5g Fat; 5g Carbs; 5g Protein

Green Chili Enchilada Casserole

When you think of Mexican food, burritos and enchiladas instantly come to mind. This chicken, green chili and cheese casserole is not only low carb but gluten free as well. This new version of a Mexican classic will quickly become a favorite in your house.

Prep time 10 minutes

Cooking time 30 minutes

Ingredients:

4 cups cauliflower florets

½ cup cream cheese, room temperature

2 cups chicken, cooked and cut into small pieces

½ cup green salsa

½ teaspoon sea salt

⅛ teaspoon freshly ground black pepper

1 cup Mexican blend cheese, grated

¼ cup sour cream

1 tablespoon cilantro, chopped course

Directions:

Heat oven to 375 degrees. Lightly grease 2 quart casserole dish.

Place the cauliflower in a medium saucepan and add just enough water to cover. Cook over medium heat about 10 minutes or till tender. Drain well and add to a medium glass bowl.

Add the cream cheese and microwave about 30 seconds. Stir to mix the cauliflower and cream cheese together.

Add the remaining ingredients to the bowl. Stir together until the ingredients are evenly mixed. Place the mixture into the prepared casserole dish.

Bake in hot oven for about 20 minutes or until the cheese is melted and the casserole is heated through. Serve.

Serves 6

Nutritional information: Serving size 1 cup

311 Calories; 18g Fat; 4g Carbs; 33g Protein

Italian Meatballs & Parmesan Pureed Cauliflower

This is a low carb version of spaghetti and meatballs. Don't be daunted by the ingredient list or number of steps, it is much simpler to prepare than it looks. The end result is a dish you can serve to impress the pickiest eater.

Prep time 15 minutes

Cooking time 30 minutes

Ingredients:

1 pound pork sausage

⅓ cup almond flour

2 tablespoons water

1 egg

1/2 cup parmesan cheese, grated, divided

¼ cup parsley, chopped fine

½ teaspoon garlic salt

¼ teaspoon pepper

3 tablespoons extra-virgin olive oil

1 clove garlic, peeled and thinly sliced

4 cups fresh spinach, rinsed, drained and loosely chopped

1 large head cauliflower, separated into small florets

2 tablespoons butter

2 tablespoons heavy cream

Salt and pepper

For the Sauce:

1 tablespoon extra-virgin olive oil

¼ cup onion, chopped fine

1 clove garlic, chopped fine

1 can tomatoes, crushed

1 cup vegetable broth

2 tablespoons heavy cream

1 teaspoon oregano, chopped fine

½ teaspoon lemon zest

Directions:

In a medium mixing bowl, combine sausage, almond flour, water, egg, ¼ cup parmesan cheese, parsley, garlic salt and pepper.

Using your hands, mix together till all of the ingredients are incorporated. Form into balls, the mixture should make at least 15 meatballs.

Heat two tablespoon of the oil in a medium skillet over medium heat. Cook the meatballs till nicely browned and cooked through. Turn them over as they cook to brown all sides. Drain on paper towel line cookie sheet.

In a separate skillet, heat one tablespoon of oil over medium high heat. Add the sliced garlic and cook about 2 minutes. Then add the spinach and cook just till it begins to wilt, about 2 minutes. Remove from heat and place into a bowl.

Place the cauliflower, butter and cream into a large sauce pan. Cook over medium heat, stirring frequently, till mixture comes to a simmer. Simmer, uncovered, 15 minutes or till cauliflower is soft.

Pour the cauliflower mixture into a blender and add the remaining ¼ parmesan cheese. Process till completely smooth and no chunks remain. Season with salt and pepper to taste.

For the sauce: In the same skillet used to cook the spinach, heat one tablespoon oil over medium high heat. Add the onion and chopped garlic and cook, stirring frequently, about 4-5 minutes or till onions are transparent.

Pour in the tomatoes and vegetable broth and bring to a simmer. Continue simmering for 10 minutes, stirring occasionally.

After about 10 minutes add the cream, oregano and lemon zest to the sauce and cook another 2-3 minutes. Remove from heat.

To serve: Layer each plate with ½ cup cauliflower, 3 meatballs, about ¼ cup spinach and top with sauce.

Serves 5

Nutritional information: Serving size 1 plate

560 Calories; 47g Fat; 10g Carbs; 25g Protein

Spanish Paella

Here is a low carb version of the classic seafood and rice dish. It tastes just like the real thing and you won't even miss the rice. If you would like to lower the carb count even more, leave out the peas.

Prep time 25 minutes

Cooking time 35 minutes

Ingredients:

1 pound chicken thighs, skinless and boneless

1 pound medium shrimp, uncooked, peeled & deveined

1 dozen mussels, cleaned

2 chorizo sausages, cut into pieces

1 medium yellow onion, chopped fine

1 green bell pepper, seeded and cut into strips

2 teaspoons garlic, chopped fine

2 tablespoon extra-virgin olive oil

1 medium head cauliflower, grated

2 teaspoon salt

1 teaspoon saffron

1/2 teaspoon pepper

1/4 teaspoon paprika

1 can diced tomatoes, drained well

1 cup frozen peas

Directions:

Heat the oven on broil. Sprinkle the chicken with a little salt and pepper on both sides.

Place in a baking dish and cook till almost done, about 4 minutes per side. Remove from oven and cool completely.

Heat one tablespoon of olive oil in a medium skillet over medium heat. Add the onion, bell pepper and garlic. Cook, stirring frequently, till the peppers are tender, about 4-5 minutes. Using a slotted spoon, remove the vegetables and put them into a medium mixing bowl.

Add the chorizo to the pan and cook no more than 2 minutes, stirring frequently. Drain off the grease and add to vegetables in the bowl.

When the chicken has cooled, cut it into small pieces and add to the bowl of chorizo and vegetables.

In a large sauce pot, heat the remaining tablespoon of oil over medium heat. Add the cauliflower and seasonings. Cook, stirring frequently about 8-10 minutes till cauliflower is almost tender.

Add the mussels and shrimp to the cauliflower and cook about 3 minutes or till the shrimp start to turn pink and mussels begin to open.

Add the vegetables and meat in the bowl along with the tomatoes and peas and stir to combine all of the ingredients. Continue cooking another 5 minutes, till all the mussels have opened and the ingredients are heated through. Serve.

Serves 6

Nutritional information: Serving size about 1 ½ cups

340 Calories; 16g Carbs; 14g Carbs; 34g Protein

Conclusion

Who knew cauliflower was so versatile? Think of cauliflower as a blank canvas waiting to be painted. Add it to your own favorite recipes to create healthier, low carb versions. It cooks up similar in texture to potatoes and rice and makes an easy, economical substitute. Whether you are following the low carb diet to lose weight, control diabetes or just eat healthier, these recipes will help you to do that. Feel free to add any of your favorite meats or veggies to create your own unique low carb meals. Just remember to stay away from processed foods and foods containing wheat flour and sugar substitutes.

51043319R00056

Made in the USA
Middletown, DE
29 June 2019